Title: "AI and Business: Shaping the Future Together"

Table of Contents:

Introduction: The Convergence of AI and Business**
    - The Evolution of AI
    - AI in the Modern Business Landscape

Chapter 1: Understanding AI: A Business Perspective**
    - What is Artificial Intelligence?
    - Key Components of AI: Machine Learning, Deep Learning, and Neural Networks
    - The AI Technology Stack

Chapter 2: AI-Driven Business Transformation**
    - Digital Transformation Through AI
    - Case Studies: AI Success Stories in Business
    - Challenges and Pitfalls in AI Integration

Chapter 3: AI and the Customer Experience**
    - Personalization and Customer Insights
    - Chatbots and Virtual Assistants
    - Predictive Analytics for Customer Retention

Chapter 4: AI in Operations and Supply Chain Management**
    - AI for Inventory Management
    - Predictive Maintenance and AI

- Autonomous Supply Chains

Chapter 5: AI in Marketing and Sales
- Targeted Advertising and Customer Segmentation
- AI-Driven Content Creation
- Sales Forecasting and Lead Scoring

Chapter 6: Ethical and Legal Considerations
- Data Privacy and Security
- Ethical AI: Bias and Fairness
- Regulatory Landscape for AI

Chapter 7: The Future of Work with AI
- Job Displacement vs. Job Creation
- AI in Workforce Management
- Skills for the Future: Preparing the Workforce

Chapter 8: Strategic Planning for AI Implementation
- Developing an AI Strategy
- Building an AI-Ready Culture
- Measuring AI Success: KPIs and Metrics

Chapter 9: Industry-Specific AI Applications
- AI in Healthcare
- AI in Finance
- AI in Retail
- AI in Manufacturing

Chapter 10: Emerging Trends and Future Directions**
 - AI and the Internet of Things (IoT)
 - Quantum Computing and AI
 - AI and Blockchain: Potential Synergies
 - The Role of AI in Sustainable Business Practices

Conclusion: Navigating the AI-Driven Future**
 - The Continuous Evolution of AI
 - Preparing for a Future with AI
 - Final Thoughts and Recommendations

DEDICATION:

To the dreamers, visionaries, and innovators who dare to push the boundaries of what is possible, this work is dedicated. It is a tribute to those who refuse to accept the status quo and instead envision a future filled with endless possibilities.

In a world where curiosity fuels progress and innovation knows no bounds, this dedication honors the relentless pursuit of knowledge and discovery. It celebrates the courage to explore the unknown and the determination to overcome obstacles in the quest for greatness.

May this dedication serve as a reminder of the power of imagination, the importance of perseverance, and the impact of collective effort. Together, let us continue to dream, innovate, and inspire as we journey into the uncharted territories of the AI-driven future.

FORWARD:

In the ever-evolving landscape of technology and innovation, we all stand at the threshold of a new era defined by the transformative power of artificial intelligence (AI). As we embark on this journey into the AI-driven future, it is with great anticipation and excitement that we present this comprehensive exploration of AI and its implications for business, society, and humanity.

Down the pages, you will discover the evolution of AI from its inception to its current state, as well as its potential to reshape industries, revolutionize workflows, and redefine human interactions. Through insightful chapters on AI applications in various sectors, strategic planning for AI implementation, and emerging trends shaping the future, this book offers a roadmap for navigating the complexities of the AI landscape.

With a forward-thinking approach, we delve into the ethical considerations, legal implications, and societal impacts of AI adoption, emphasizing the importance of responsible AI development and deployment. By highlighting best practices, case studies, and real-world examples, we aim to empower readers to harness the full potential of AI while addressing challenges and ensuring inclusivity and equity.

As we stand on the cusp of unprecedented technological advancement, the future holds limitless possibilities for those bold enough to embrace innovation and adapt to change. It is our sincere hope that this book serves as a valuable resource and inspiration for all who seek to navigate the AI-driven future with knowledge, wisdom, and foresight.

Forward into the future, where AI and human ingenuity converge to create a world of endless opportunity and boundless potential.

[Kenneth Christopher]

ACKNOWLEDGMENT:

I would like to express my sincere gratitude to all those who have contributed to the creation of this book on AI and its impact on business.

First and foremost, I will love to extend my deepest appreciation to the researchers, scholars, and experts in the field of artificial intelligence whose pioneering work has paved the way for advancements in this rapidly evolving field. Their insights, expertise, and dedication to pushing the boundaries of AI have inspired and informed the content of this book.

I also acknowledge the support and guidance of my colleagues, mentors, and industry partners who have provided valuable feedback, encouragement, and assistance throughout the writing process of this book. Their input and expertise have been instrumental in shaping the structure, content, and relevance of this book.

Furthermore, I will like to thank the organizations and institutions that have generously shared their knowledge, resources, and case studies, enabling me to provide comprehensive coverage of AI applications across various industries.

Last but not least, I express my profound gratitude to my families, friends, and loved ones for their unwavering support, understanding, and patience during the countless hours spent researching, writing, and revising this book.

It is with heartfelt appreciation that I acknowledge the collective effort and collaboration of all those who have contributed to the realization of this project. May this book serve as a valuable resource and inspiration for all who seek to navigate the AI-driven future with knowledge, wisdom, and foresight. Thank you all and God continue to bless you all.

[Kenneth Christopher]

Introduction: The Convergence of AI and Business

The Evolution of AI

Artificial Intelligence (AI) has come a long way from its conceptual roots in the mid-20th century to becoming an integral part of the 21st-century business landscape. Initially, AI was the domain of academics and researchers, focusing on theories and algorithms that could mimic human intelligence. Early AI systems were limited by the computational power and data availability of their time. However, with the advent of powerful computing technologies, big data, and advanced algorithms, AI has evolved into a robust and dynamic field that drives innovation across industries.

In its current form, AI encompasses a wide range of technologies, including machine learning, deep learning, natural language processing, and computer vision. These technologies enable machines to learn from data, recognize patterns, make decisions, and even perform tasks that typically require human intelligence. The progression from simple rule-based systems to sophisticated neural networks has opened up new possibilities for AI applications, transforming how businesses operate and compete.

AI in the Modern Business Landscape

Today, AI is not just a futuristic concept but a reality that is reshaping businesses around the world. From enhancing customer experiences to optimizing operations and driving innovation, AI's impact is profound and far-reaching. Companies across various sectors are leveraging AI to gain a competitive edge, improve efficiency, and create value for their stakeholders.

1. **Enhanced Customer Experience**: AI-powered tools like chatbots, virtual assistants, and personalized recommendation systems are revolutionizing customer

service. By understanding and anticipating customer needs, businesses can provide tailored experiences that foster loyalty and satisfaction.

2. **Operational Efficiency**: AI-driven automation and predictive analytics enable companies to streamline processes, reduce costs, and enhance productivity. In supply chain management, for instance, AI helps in forecasting demand, optimizing inventory levels, and ensuring timely deliveries.

3. **Innovation and Product Development**: AI facilitates the development of new products and services by analyzing market trends, consumer behavior, and emerging technologies. This insight-driven approach helps businesses stay ahead of the curve and meet evolving customer demands.

4. **Decision-Making**: AI enhances decision-making by providing data-driven insights and real-time analysis. Executives can make informed choices based on predictive models and scenario planning, reducing risks and maximizing opportunities.

The Transformative Potential of AI

As AI continues to advance, its potential to transform business practices grows exponentially. The convergence of AI with other emerging technologies, such as the Internet of Things (IoT), blockchain, and quantum computing, promises to create new paradigms in the business world. For example, AI and IoT together enable smart manufacturing, where interconnected devices and sensors collect and analyze data to optimize production processes in real-time.

Moreover, AI's role in sustainable business practices is becoming increasingly significant. By optimizing resource usage, reducing waste, and enhancing energy efficiency, AI helps companies adopt environmentally friendly practices that align with global sustainability goals.

However, the journey of integrating AI into business is not without challenges. Ethical considerations, data privacy concerns, and the need for regulatory compliance are critical issues that companies must navigate. Ensuring that AI systems are fair, transparent, and unbiased is essential to build trust and avoid potential pitfalls.

Conclusion

The convergence of AI and business marks a transformative era where intelligent systems drive growth, efficiency, and innovation. As we delve deeper into this book, we will explore how AI is reshaping various aspects of business, from customer engagement and operational efficiency to strategic decision-making and industry-specific applications. By understanding and leveraging AI, businesses can not only stay competitive but also lead in an increasingly digital and data-driven world.

The Evolution of AI

Early Beginnings and Theoretical Foundations

Artificial Intelligence (AI) has a rich history that dates back to the mid-20th century when the concept of machines capable of mimicking human intelligence first emerged. The term "artificial intelligence" was coined in 1956 during the Dartmouth Conference, organized by John McCarthy, Marvin Minsky, Nathaniel Rochester, and Claude Shannon. This event is widely considered the birth of AI as a field of study.

In the early days, AI research focused on symbolic AI, also known as "good old-fashioned AI" (GOFAI). Researchers developed systems that used logical reasoning and symbolic manipulation to solve problems and perform tasks. Early successes included programs that could play chess, solve mathematical problems, and prove theorems. However, these systems were limited by their inability to handle real-world complexity and ambiguity.

The Advent of Machine Learning

The 1980s and 1990s saw a shift from symbolic AI to machine learning, a subfield of AI that emphasizes the development of algorithms that allow computers to learn from and make predictions based on data. Machine learning algorithms, such as decision trees, support vector machines, and neural networks, began to gain traction. These algorithms were more flexible and could adapt to a wider range of problems than symbolic AI.

During this period, the concept of neural networks, inspired by the structure and function of the human brain, started to gain attention. However, early neural networks, such as the perception, faced limitations due to computational constraints and the lack of large datasets. As a result, AI research experienced periods of enthusiasm followed by "AI winters"—times of reduced funding and interest due to unmet expectations.

The Rise of Big Data and Deep Learning

The turn of the 21st century marked a new era for AI, driven by the explosion of big data, advances in computational power, and breakthroughs in algorithms.

The availability of massive datasets and powerful GPUs enabled researchers to train more complex models. This period saw the resurgence of neural networks, particularly deep learning, which involves training multi-layered neural networks on large amounts of data.

Deep learning achieved significant milestones, particularly in the fields of computer vision and natural language processing. Convolution neural networks (CNNs) revolutionized image recognition, leading to remarkable progress in areas such as facial recognition, autonomous driving, and medical imaging. Recurrent neural networks (RNNs) and transformers brought advancements in language translation, sentiment analysis, and chatbots.

AI in the Modern Era

Today, AI is a ubiquitous presence across various sectors, from healthcare and finance to retail and entertainment. The integration of AI into everyday applications has transformed how we live and work. Key developments include:

1. **Natural Language Processing (NLP)**: AI systems can now understand and generate human language with high accuracy. Technologies like GPT-3 and its

successors can write essays, create content, and assist in customer service.

2. **Computer Vision**: AI algorithms can analyze and interpret visual data from the world around us. Applications include facial recognition, object detection, and medical diagnosis.

3. **Reinforcement Learning**: This area focuses on training AI agents to make decisions by rewarding them for desirable actions. It has been applied to complex tasks such as game playing, robotics, and autonomous vehicles.

4. **AI in Everyday Devices**: From smartphones to smart home devices, AI enhances the functionality and user experience. Voice assistants like Siri and Alexa rely on AI to interact with users and perform tasks.

5. **Industry Applications**: AI is revolutionizing industries by improving efficiency, reducing costs, and enabling innovation. In healthcare, AI assists in diagnosing diseases and personalizing treatment plans. In finance, it aids in fraud detection and algorithmic trading.

Challenges and Ethical Considerations

Despite its rapid advancement, AI faces several challenges and ethical considerations:

- **Bias and Fairness**: AI systems can inherit biases from the data they are trained on, leading to unfair or discriminatory outcomes. Ensuring fairness and accountability in AI is a critical area of research.

- **Transparency and Explainability**: Many AI models, especially deep learning systems, are often considered "black boxes" because their decision-making processes are not easily understood. Improving transparency and explainability is essential for trust and adoption.

- **Privacy and Security**: The use of AI involves handling large amounts of data, raising concerns about data privacy and security. Implementing robust measures to protect sensitive information is crucial.

- **Regulation and Governance**: As AI becomes more pervasive, the need for regulatory frameworks and ethical guidelines grows. Governments and organizations must work together to develop standards that ensure the responsible use of AI.

The Future of AI

The future of AI holds immense promise, with ongoing research exploring new frontiers such as quantum computing, neuromorphic engineering, and general AI. AI's potential to solve complex global challenges, such as climate change, healthcare, and education, continues to inspire researchers and innovators.

As AI evolves, its integration with other emerging technologies, such as the Internet of Things (IoT) and blockchain, will unlock new possibilities and drive further transformation across industries. The journey of AI is far from over, and its continued evolution will shape the future of business and society in profound ways.

AI in the Modern Business Landscape

Introduction

In the modern business landscape, Artificial Intelligence (AI) has transitioned from a futuristic concept to a crucial component that drives innovation, efficiency, and competitive advantage. As AI technologies become more sophisticated and accessible, they are reshaping how businesses operate, interact with customers, and develop new products and services. This chapter explores the profound impact of

AI across various business functions and industries, highlighting key applications, benefits, and challenges.

Enhanced Customer Experience

AI is revolutionizing customer experience by enabling businesses to provide personalized, timely, and efficient interactions. Key applications include:

1. **Personalization**: AI algorithms analyze customer data to deliver personalized recommendations, offers, and content. Companies like Amazon and Netflix use AI to suggest products and shows based on user behavior and preferences, enhancing customer satisfaction and loyalty.

2. **Chatbots and Virtual Assistants**: AI-powered chatbots and virtual assistants provide instant customer support, handle inquiries, and perform tasks such as booking appointments or processing orders. These tools reduce response times and improve service efficiency. For example, companies like Sephora and H&M use chatbots to assist customers with product information and purchase decisions.

3. **Predictive Analytics**: AI-driven predictive analytics help businesses anticipate customer needs and behaviors. By analyzing historical data, AI can

predict future trends, enabling companies to proactively address customer demands and reduce churn. For instance, telecom companies use predictive models to identify customers at risk of leaving and offer targeted retention strategies.

Operational Efficiency

AI enhances operational efficiency by automating processes, optimizing resource allocation, and improving decision-making. Key applications include:

1. **Automation**: AI-driven automation reduces the need for manual intervention in repetitive tasks. Robotic Process Automation (RPA) uses AI to automate workflows, such as data entry, invoicing, and compliance reporting. Companies like UiPath and Automation Anywhere provide RPA solutions that streamline operations and reduce costs.

2. **Supply Chain Optimization**: AI improves supply chain management by enhancing demand forecasting, inventory management, and logistics planning. Machine learning models analyze sales data, market trends, and external factors to optimize inventory levels and reduce stockouts or overstock situations. Companies like DHL and FedEx use AI to optimize delivery routes and improve logistics efficiency.

3. **Predictive Maintenance**: AI-powered predictive maintenance helps businesses prevent equipment failures and minimize downtime. By analyzing sensor data and identifying patterns, AI can predict when machinery is likely to fail and schedule maintenance accordingly. Manufacturers like Siemens and General Electric use AI for predictive maintenance, increasing equipment reliability and lifespan.

Innovation and Product Development

AI accelerates innovation and product development by providing insights into market trends, consumer behavior, and technological advancements. Key applications include:

1. **Market Research**: AI tools analyze vast amounts of data from social media, surveys, and market reports to identify emerging trends and consumer preferences. This enables businesses to make data-driven decisions and stay ahead of the competition. For example, Unilever uses AI to analyze social media trends and develop new products that resonate with consumers.

2. **Product Design and Development**: AI-driven design tools assist in creating new products by generating design options based on specified criteria

and learning from historical data. These tools enable faster prototyping and testing, reducing time-to-market. Companies like Autodesk use AI for generative design, producing innovative and efficient product designs.

3. **Innovation Management**: AI helps businesses manage the innovation process by identifying promising ideas, optimizing project portfolios, and predicting the success of new ventures. AI-driven platforms like Spigit and IdeaScale facilitate idea generation and evaluation, fostering a culture of innovation within organizations.

Decision-Making

AI enhances decision-making by providing real-time insights, predictive analytics, and scenario planning. Key applications include:

1. **Data-Driven Insights**: AI systems analyze large datasets to uncover patterns and generate actionable insights. These insights inform strategic decisions, such as market entry, product launches, and pricing strategies. For instance, retailers use AI to analyze sales data and optimize pricing strategies based on consumer demand and competitor actions.

2. **Predictive Models**: AI-driven predictive models help businesses forecast future outcomes and make informed decisions. In finance, AI models predict stock prices, credit risks, and market trends, enabling better investment and risk management decisions. Companies like Goldman Sachs and JPMorgan Chase use AI for financial forecasting and trading.

3. **Scenario Planning**: AI supports scenario planning by simulating different business scenarios and evaluating their potential impacts. This helps executives assess risks, identify opportunities, and develop contingency plans. For example, oil and gas companies use AI to model the impact of fluctuating oil prices on their operations and profitability.

Industry-Specific Applications

AI's impact varies across industries, with tailored applications addressing specific challenges and opportunities. Key examples include:

1. **Healthcare**: AI enhances diagnostic accuracy, personalizes treatment plans, and improves patient care. Machine learning algorithms analyze medical images, genetic data, and patient records to assist in diagnosing diseases and predicting health outcomes.

Companies like IBM Watson Health and Google Health use AI to advance medical research and patient care.

2. **Finance**: AI improves fraud detection, credit scoring, and trading strategies. By analyzing transaction data and identifying anomalies, AI systems detect fraudulent activities in real-time. Financial institutions use AI-driven credit scoring models to assess loan applications more accurately. AI-powered trading algorithms analyze market data and execute trades at optimal times, maximizing returns.

3. **Retail**: AI transforms the retail experience by enhancing customer engagement, optimizing inventory, and streamlining supply chains. Retailers use AI to personalize shopping experiences, recommend products, and predict demand. AI-driven systems improve inventory management by forecasting sales and reducing stockouts. Companies like Walmart and Alibaba leverage AI to enhance their retail operations.

4. **Manufacturing**: AI optimizes production processes, improves quality control, and reduces costs. Machine learning models analyze production data to identify inefficiencies and suggest improvements. AI-driven quality control systems detect defects and ensure product consistency. Manufacturers use AI to optimize production schedules and reduce waste.

Challenges and Ethical Considerations

While AI offers significant benefits, businesses must address several challenges and ethical considerations:

- **Data Quality and Privacy**: Ensuring high-quality data is essential for effective AI implementation. Businesses must also protect customer data and comply with privacy regulations, such as GDPR and CCPA.

- **Bias and Fairness**: AI systems can inherit biases from the data they are trained on, leading to unfair or discriminatory outcomes. Companies must implement measures to detect and mitigate bias in AI models.

- **Transparency and Explainability**: Many AI models, especially deep learning systems, operate as "black boxes" with complex decision-making processes. Enhancing transparency and explainability is crucial for building trust and accountability.

- **Regulation and Governance**: The increasing use of AI necessitates regulatory frameworks and ethical guidelines. Businesses must stay informed about regulatory developments and adopt best practices for responsible AI use.

AI is transforming the modern business landscape by enhancing customer experiences, improving operational efficiency, driving innovation, and supporting data-driven decision-making. As AI technologies continue to evolve, businesses must navigate challenges related to data quality, bias, transparency, and regulation to fully harness AI's potential. By leveraging AI strategically, companies can achieve sustained growth and maintain a competitive edge in an increasingly digital and dynamic marketplace.

Chapter 1: Understanding AI: A Business Perspective

What is Artificial Intelligence?

Artificial Intelligence (AI) refers to the development of computer systems that can perform tasks typically requiring human intelligence. These tasks include learning, reasoning, problem-solving, perception, and language understanding. AI systems are designed to simulate human cognitive processes, enabling them to interpret data, recognize patterns, and make decisions.

AI can be broadly categorized into two types:

1. **Narrow AI (Weak AI)**: These systems are designed to perform specific tasks or solve particular problems. Examples include voice assistants like Siri and Alexa, recommendation systems on Netflix and Amazon, and autonomous vehicles. Narrow AI excels in its designated area but cannot perform tasks outside its scope.

2. **General AI (Strong AI)**: This theoretical form of AI would possess the ability to understand, learn, and apply intelligence across a wide range of tasks, similar to human intelligence. While significant advancements have been made in narrow AI, general AI remains a goal for future research and development.

Key Components of AI: Machine Learning, Deep Learning, and Neural Networks

Understanding the key components of AI is crucial for businesses looking to integrate AI into their operations. The main components include:

1. **Machine Learning (ML)**:
    - **Definition**: Machine Learning is a subset of AI that involves the development of algorithms that enable computers to learn from and make predictions based on data.
    - **Types of Machine Learning**:

- **Supervised Learning**: The algorithm is trained on labeled data, meaning the input data is paired with the correct output. Examples include spam detection in emails and fraud detection in financial transactions.
   - **Unsupervised Learning**: The algorithm is trained on unlabeled data and must find patterns and relationships within the data. Examples include customer segmentation and anomaly detection.
   - **Reinforcement Learning**: The algorithm learns by interacting with an environment and receiving feedback in the form of rewards or penalties. Examples include game playing and robotic control.

2. **Deep Learning**:
   - **Definition**: Deep Learning is a subset of machine learning that uses neural networks with many layers (hence "deep") to model complex patterns in large datasets.
   - **Applications**: Deep learning has been particularly successful in areas such as image recognition, natural language processing, and speech recognition. Examples include facial recognition systems and language translation services.

3. **Neural Networks**:
   - **Definition**: Neural Networks are computational models inspired by the human brain's structure and

function. They consist of interconnected nodes (neurons) that process and transmit information.
   - **Types of Neural Networks**:
     - **Feedforward Neural Networks**: Information moves in one direction from input to output. They are used in applications like handwriting recognition.
     - **Convolutional Neural Networks (CNNs)**: These networks are designed to process grid-like data, such as images. They are widely used in image and video recognition.
     - **Recurrent Neural Networks (RNNs)**: These networks are designed to handle sequential data, such as time series or text. They are used in applications like language modeling and machine translation.

The AI Technology Stack

The AI technology stack comprises various tools, frameworks, and platforms that support the development and deployment of AI solutions. Key components of the AI technology stack include:

1. **Data Collection and Storage**:
   - **Data Sources**: AI systems require large volumes of data, which can be collected from various sources, including sensors, databases, social media, and enterprise systems.

- **Data Storage**: Efficient data storage solutions, such as cloud storage, data lakes, and data warehouses, are essential for managing and accessing the vast amounts of data needed for AI.

2. **Data Processing and Management**:
   - **Data Cleaning and Preprocessing**: Raw data often requires cleaning and preprocessing to remove noise, handle missing values, and transform it into a suitable format for analysis.
   - **Data Management**: Tools for managing data, such as database management systems (DBMS) and data integration platforms, are crucial for ensuring data quality and accessibility.

3. **AI Frameworks and Libraries**:
   - **Popular Frameworks**: Frameworks such as TensorFlow, PyTorch, and Keras provide pre-built components and tools for developing AI models.
   - **Libraries**: Libraries like scikit-learn, OpenCV, and NLTK offer specialized functions for machine learning, computer vision, and natural language processing.

4. **Model Development and Training**:
   - **Development Environments**: Integrated development environments (IDEs) like Jupyter

Notebooks and Visual Studio Code facilitate the development and experimentation of AI models.
   - **Training Infrastructure**: Powerful computing resources, including GPUs and TPUs, are required for training complex AI models. Cloud-based services like AWS, Google Cloud, and Azure provide scalable infrastructure for model training.

5. **Deployment and Integration**:
   - **Model Deployment**: Tools and platforms for deploying AI models into production environments, such as Docker, Kubernetes, and TensorFlow Serving, enable seamless integration with existing systems.
   - **APIs and Microservices**: AI models can be exposed as APIs or microservices, allowing other applications and systems to leverage AI capabilities.

6. **Monitoring and Maintenance**:
   - **Performance Monitoring**: Tools for monitoring the performance of AI models in production, such as Prometheus and Grafana, help ensure models continue to perform accurately and efficiently.
   - **Model Maintenance**: Regular updates and retraining of models are necessary to maintain their relevance and accuracy as new data becomes available.

Understanding the fundamentals of AI, including its key components and technology stack, is essential for businesses looking to leverage AI for strategic advantage. By grasping the concepts of machine learning, deep learning, and neural networks, and familiarizing themselves with the AI technology stack, business leaders can make informed decisions about integrating AI into their operations. The following chapters will delve deeper into specific applications of AI in business, exploring how companies can harness its power to drive innovation, efficiency, and growth.

Chapter 2: AI-Driven Business Transformation

Introduction

Artificial Intelligence (AI) is not just a technological advancement; it is a catalyst for profound business transformation. By leveraging AI, companies can revolutionize their operations, strategies, and market positions. This chapter explores how AI drives business transformation, highlighting its impact on various sectors, key success stories, and the strategies businesses can adopt to harness AI's potential.

The Impact of AI Across Industries

AI's transformative power spans across multiple industries, reshaping processes, products, and services. Here are some of the key sectors experiencing significant AI-driven transformation:

1. **Healthcare**:
   - **Diagnostics and Treatment**: AI algorithms analyze medical images, genetic data, and patient histories to assist in diagnosing diseases and personalizing treatment plans. For instance, IBM Watson Health uses AI to identify cancer treatment options.
   - **Operational Efficiency**: AI streamlines hospital operations, from optimizing staff schedules to managing patient flow. Predictive analytics forecast patient admissions, helping allocate resources efficiently.

2. **Finance**:
   - **Fraud Detection**: AI systems detect fraudulent activities by analyzing transaction patterns and flagging anomalies in real-time. Companies like PayPal use AI to enhance security and protect customer accounts.
   - **Investment Strategies**: AI-driven predictive models analyze market data to inform trading strategies and investment decisions. Hedge funds and financial institutions leverage AI for algorithmic trading and risk management.

3. **Retail**:
   - **Personalized Shopping**: AI algorithms recommend products based on customer behavior and preferences, enhancing the shopping experience. E-commerce giants like Amazon use AI to drive sales and improve customer satisfaction.
   - **Inventory Management**: AI optimizes inventory levels by predicting demand and adjusting stock accordingly. Retailers reduce waste and ensure product availability, improving operational efficiency.

4. **Manufacturing**:
   - **Predictive Maintenance**: AI monitors equipment performance and predicts failures, scheduling maintenance before breakdowns occur. This approach reduces downtime and extends machinery lifespan, as seen in companies like Siemens.
   - **Quality Control**: AI-powered vision systems inspect products for defects, ensuring consistent quality. Manufacturers like Toyota use AI to maintain high standards and reduce waste.

5. **Marketing and Sales**:
   - **Customer Insights**: AI analyzes customer data to uncover insights and trends, informing targeted marketing campaigns. Businesses like Coca-Cola use AI to tailor their advertising strategies and increase ROI.

- **Sales Automation**: AI-driven tools automate sales processes, from lead generation to follow-ups, enhancing efficiency and effectiveness. CRM systems like Salesforce integrate AI to support sales teams.

Case Studies: Success Stories of AI-Driven Transformation

Examining real-world examples provides valuable insights into how AI drives business transformation:

1. **Netflix**:
   - **Personalized Recommendations**: Netflix uses AI to analyze viewing habits and recommend content tailored to individual users. This personalization increases viewer engagement and retention, driving subscription growth.
   - **Content Creation**: AI analyzes viewer preferences and market trends to inform content creation decisions. Netflix invests in producing shows and movies that align with audience interests, enhancing its competitive edge.

2. **UPS**:
   - **Route Optimization**: UPS uses AI and advanced analytics to optimize delivery routes, reducing fuel consumption and improving delivery times. The ORION system analyzes data from multiple

sources to determine the most efficient routes, saving millions of dollars annually.
   - **Predictive Maintenance**: AI monitors vehicle performance and predicts maintenance needs, reducing breakdowns and ensuring fleet reliability. This proactive approach enhances operational efficiency and customer satisfaction.

3. **Zara**:
   - **Demand Forecasting**: Zara employs AI to forecast fashion trends and customer demand, enabling agile inventory management. This capability allows Zara to quickly respond to market changes and minimize overproduction.
   - **Supply Chain Efficiency**: AI streamlines Zara's supply chain, optimizing everything from manufacturing to logistics. The result is a more responsive and efficient operation that supports rapid product turnover.

Strategies for AI-Driven Business Transformation

To successfully integrate AI into business operations, companies should consider the following strategies:

1. **Develop a Clear AI Strategy**:
   - **Set Objectives**: Define clear goals for AI implementation, such as improving customer

experience, increasing efficiency, or driving innovation. Align AI initiatives with overall business objectives to ensure coherence and focus.
   - **Prioritize Use Cases**: Identify high-impact use cases where AI can deliver significant value. Start with pilot projects to test and refine AI applications before scaling up.

2. **Invest in Data Infrastructure**:
   - **Data Collection**: Implement robust data collection processes to gather high-quality, relevant data. Ensure data is clean, structured, and accessible for AI analysis.
   - **Data Integration**: Integrate data from various sources to create a comprehensive dataset. Use data lakes or warehouses to manage and store data efficiently.

3. **Build AI Expertise**:
   - **Talent Acquisition**: Hire AI experts, including data scientists, machine learning engineers, and AI strategists. Foster a culture of continuous learning and development to keep pace with AI advancements.
   - **Collaboration**: Partner with AI vendors, research institutions, and industry experts to leverage external expertise and accelerate AI adoption.

4. **Ensure Ethical AI Practices**:

- **Bias Mitigation**: Implement measures to detect and mitigate biases in AI models. Use diverse datasets and regularly audit AI systems to ensure fairness and accuracy.
   - **Transparency and Explainability**: Develop AI systems that are transparent and explainable, enabling stakeholders to understand and trust AI decisions. Prioritize models that provide clear insights into their decision-making processes.

5. **Foster a Culture of Innovation**:
   - **Encourage Experimentation**: Promote a culture that encourages experimentation and innovation. Provide resources and support for employees to explore new AI applications and ideas.
   - **Agile Methodologies**: Adopt agile methodologies to enable rapid development, testing, and iteration of AI projects. This approach allows businesses to quickly adapt to changing market conditions and technological advancements.

Challenges and Considerations

While AI offers significant benefits, businesses must navigate several challenges:

- **Cost and Complexity**: Implementing AI solutions can be costly and complex, requiring substantial investments in technology, infrastructure, and talent. Businesses must carefully assess the ROI of AI projects and manage resources effectively.

- **Change Management**: AI-driven transformation often involves significant changes to existing processes and workflows. Effective change management strategies are essential to ensure smooth adoption and minimize resistance from employees.

- **Regulatory Compliance**: Businesses must comply with regulations related to data privacy, security, and AI ethics. Staying informed about regulatory developments and implementing robust compliance measures is crucial.

- **Scalability**: Scaling AI solutions from pilot projects to enterprise-wide implementations can be challenging. Businesses must develop strategies for scaling AI technologies while maintaining performance and reliability.

AI-driven business transformation offers immense potential for companies to innovate, enhance efficiency, and gain a competitive edge. By understanding AI's impact across industries, learning from success stories, and adopting strategic approaches, businesses can harness AI's power to drive meaningful change. As AI technologies continue to evolve, staying agile and adaptable will be key to navigating the challenges and maximizing the opportunities presented by AI.

Chapter 3: AI and the Customer Experience

Introduction

In the digital age, customer experience (CX) is a critical differentiator for businesses. AI is transforming how companies interact with customers, offering personalized, efficient, and proactive experiences. This chapter delves into the various ways AI enhances customer experience, exploring key applications, benefits, challenges, and strategies for successful implementation.

The Role of AI in Enhancing Customer Experience

AI technologies enable businesses to deliver superior customer experiences by leveraging data-driven insights and automating customer interactions. Key AI applications in customer experience include:

1. **Personalization**:
   - **Recommendation Engines**: AI algorithms analyze customer behavior and preferences to

recommend products, services, or content tailored to individual users. For example, Amazon's recommendation system drives a significant portion of its sales by suggesting relevant products to customers.
   - **Dynamic Pricing**: AI adjusts pricing in real-time based on demand, customer profiles, and market conditions. Airlines and e-commerce platforms use dynamic pricing to optimize revenue and offer competitive prices.

2. **Customer Support**:
   - **Chatbots and Virtual Assistants**: AI-powered chatbots provide instant responses to customer queries, handle common issues, and assist with tasks such as booking appointments or processing orders. Companies like H&M and Sephora use chatbots to enhance customer service and engagement.
   - **Automated Email Responses**: AI systems can automatically respond to customer emails, categorize inquiries, and escalate issues to human agents when necessary. This reduces response times and improves customer satisfaction.

3. **Predictive Analytics**:
   - **Customer Behavior Prediction**: AI analyzes historical data to predict future customer behaviors, such as purchasing patterns, churn likelihood, and product preferences. Retailers use predictive analytics

to personalize marketing campaigns and improve retention.
   - **Sentiment Analysis**: AI algorithms analyze customer feedback, social media posts, and reviews to gauge sentiment and identify areas for improvement. Companies use sentiment analysis to monitor brand reputation and address customer concerns proactively.

4. **Voice and Image Recognition**:
   - **Voice Assistants**: AI-powered voice assistants like Google Assistant and Amazon Alexa provide a hands-free, interactive experience for customers, helping them with tasks, providing information, and making purchases.
   - **Image Recognition**: AI enables visual search capabilities, allowing customers to upload images to find similar products. Retailers like ASOS use image recognition to enhance the shopping experience and simplify product discovery.

Benefits of AI in Customer Experience

Implementing AI in customer experience offers several benefits:

1. **Increased Customer Satisfaction**: AI enables personalized, efficient, and responsive interactions, leading to higher customer satisfaction and loyalty.

Tailored recommendations and quick resolutions to issues enhance the overall customer experience.

2. **Operational Efficiency**: AI automates routine tasks and handles large volumes of customer inquiries, freeing up human agents to focus on more complex issues. This improves operational efficiency and reduces costs.

3. **Data-Driven Insights**: AI provides valuable insights into customer preferences, behaviors, and sentiment. Businesses can use these insights to refine their strategies, improve products and services, and anticipate customer needs.

4. **Scalability**: AI systems can handle increasing volumes of customer interactions without compromising quality. This scalability is crucial for businesses looking to expand their customer base and maintain high service standards.

Challenges and Considerations

Despite its advantages, integrating AI into customer experience poses several challenges:

1. **Data Privacy and Security**: Collecting and analyzing customer data raises concerns about privacy and security. Businesses must ensure compliance with data protection regulations and implement robust security measures to safeguard customer information.

2. **Bias and Fairness**: AI systems can inherit biases from the data they are trained on, leading to unfair or discriminatory outcomes. Companies must regularly audit AI models and use diverse datasets to mitigate bias.

3. **Customer Trust**: Building trust in AI systems is essential for customer acceptance. Businesses need to ensure transparency in AI decision-making processes and provide clear explanations for AI-driven actions.

4. **Integration with Existing Systems**: Integrating AI with existing customer relationship management (CRM) systems and other business tools can be complex and require significant resources. Companies must plan for seamless integration to avoid disruptions.

Strategies for Implementing AI in Customer Experience

To successfully implement AI in customer experience, businesses should consider the following strategies:

1. **Define Clear Objectives: Establish clear goals for AI implementation, such as improving response times, increasing personalization, or enhancing customer satisfaction. Align AI initiatives with overall business objectives to ensure coherence and focus.

2. **Invest in High-Quality Data**: Ensure the availability of high-quality, relevant data for training AI models. Implement robust data collection, cleaning, and management processes to maintain data integrity.

3. **Focus on Customer-Centric Use Cases**: Prioritize AI use cases that directly impact customer experience, such as chatbots, personalized recommendations, and predictive analytics. Start with pilot projects to test and refine AI applications before scaling up.

4. **Enhance Transparency and Explainability**: Develop AI systems that are transparent and explainable, enabling customers to understand how AI decisions are made. Provide clear information about the benefits and limitations of AI to build trust.

5. **Ensure Ethical AI Practices**: Implement measures to detect and mitigate biases in AI models. Use diverse datasets and regularly audit AI systems to ensure fairness and accuracy. Establish ethical

guidelines for AI use and comply with relevant regulations.

6. **Train and Support Employees**: Provide training and support for employees to help them understand and leverage AI tools effectively. Foster a culture of innovation and continuous learning to keep pace with AI advancements.

7. **Monitor and Iterate**: Continuously monitor the performance of AI systems and gather feedback from customers and employees. Use this feedback to make iterative improvements and ensure AI solutions remain relevant and effective.

AI is revolutionizing customer experience by enabling personalized, efficient, and proactive interactions. By leveraging AI technologies such as chatbots, predictive analytics, and recommendation engines, businesses can enhance customer satisfaction, improve operational efficiency, and gain valuable insights. However, successful implementation requires careful consideration of data privacy, bias mitigation, transparency, and integration challenges. By adopting strategic approaches and focusing on customer-centric use cases, businesses can harness AI's potential to drive meaningful improvements in customer experience and achieve a competitive advantage.

Chapter 4: AI in Operations and Supply Chain Management

Introduction

Artificial Intelligence (AI) is transforming operations and supply chain management by enhancing efficiency, accuracy, and responsiveness. This chapter explores how AI is revolutionizing various aspects of operations and supply chains, providing detailed insights into key applications, benefits, challenges, and best practices for successful AI integration.

The Role of AI in Operations and Supply Chain Management

AI technologies are increasingly being integrated into operations and supply chain management to optimize processes, reduce costs, and improve decision-making. Key AI applications in this area include:

1. **Demand Forecasting**:
   - **Predictive Analytics**: AI analyzes historical sales data, market trends, and external factors to predict future demand. This enables businesses to make informed decisions about inventory levels,

production schedules, and procurement. For example, Walmart uses AI to forecast demand and manage inventory, reducing stockouts and excess inventory.

2. **Inventory Management**:
   - **Automated Inventory Tracking**: AI systems monitor inventory levels in real-time, providing accurate data on stock availability. Automated alerts and reorder recommendations help maintain optimal inventory levels. Companies like Amazon use AI to manage vast inventories across multiple warehouses, ensuring timely replenishment and minimizing carrying costs.
   - **Just-in-Time (JIT) Inventory**: AI supports JIT inventory systems by predicting demand and coordinating with suppliers to deliver components as needed, reducing storage costs and waste.

3. **Supply Chain Optimization**:
   - **Route Optimization**: AI algorithms analyze traffic patterns, weather conditions, and delivery constraints to determine the most efficient delivery routes. This reduces transportation costs and improves delivery times. UPS's ORION system, for instance, optimizes delivery routes to save millions in fuel costs.
   - **Supplier Management**: AI evaluates supplier performance, monitors risks, and forecasts supply disruptions, helping businesses maintain resilient and

efficient supply chains. AI-driven platforms like Llamasoft assist companies in managing supplier relationships and mitigating risks.

4. **Production Planning**:
    - **Predictive Maintenance**: AI predicts equipment failures and schedules maintenance proactively, reducing downtime and extending machinery lifespan. Manufacturers like General Electric use AI to monitor equipment health and optimize maintenance schedules.
    - **Quality Control**: AI-powered vision systems and sensors inspect products for defects during production, ensuring consistent quality. This reduces waste and rework, as seen in companies like Toyota.

5. **Warehouse Automation**:
    - **Robotics and Autonomous Systems**: AI-driven robots and autonomous vehicles handle tasks such as picking, packing, and transporting goods within warehouses. This increases efficiency and reduces labor costs. Amazon's fulfillment centers extensively use robots to streamline warehouse operations.
    - **Smart Warehousing**: AI optimizes warehouse layouts and storage systems, improving space utilization and reducing retrieval times.

Benefits of AI in Operations and Supply Chain Management

Implementing AI in operations and supply chain management offers numerous benefits:

1. **Increased Efficiency**: AI automates routine tasks, optimizes processes, and enhances decision-making, leading to significant efficiency gains. This results in faster production cycles, streamlined logistics, and reduced operational costs.

2. **Enhanced Accuracy**: AI systems provide accurate demand forecasts, inventory data, and supply chain insights, reducing errors and improving planning accuracy. This minimizes stockouts, overstock situations, and production delays.

3. **Cost Savings**: By optimizing inventory levels, reducing waste, and improving resource utilization, AI helps businesses achieve substantial cost savings. Predictive maintenance and efficient logistics further contribute to cost reduction.

4. **Improved Responsiveness**: AI enables real-time monitoring and analysis of supply chain activities, allowing businesses to respond quickly to changes in demand, supply disruptions, and other external factors.

This agility is crucial for maintaining competitive advantage in dynamic markets.

5. **Better Risk Management**: AI identifies potential risks in the supply chain, such as supplier reliability issues, transportation delays, and demand fluctuations. Proactive risk management helps businesses mitigate disruptions and maintain continuity.

Challenges and Considerations

Despite its benefits, integrating AI into operations and supply chain management presents several challenges:

1. **Data Quality and Availability**: AI systems rely on high-quality, comprehensive data to function effectively. Ensuring data accuracy, completeness, and consistency is essential but can be challenging, especially for businesses with disparate data sources.

2. **Integration with Legacy Systems**: Many companies operate with legacy systems that may not be compatible with AI technologies. Integrating AI with existing infrastructure can be complex and require significant investment.

3. **Scalability**: Scaling AI solutions from pilot projects to full-scale implementations can be difficult. Businesses must develop strategies to scale AI technologies while maintaining performance and reliability.

4. **Talent and Expertise**: Implementing and managing AI systems requires specialized skills in data science, machine learning, and AI engineering. Finding and retaining qualified talent can be a significant challenge.

5. **Ethical and Regulatory Considerations**: Businesses must ensure that their AI applications comply with regulatory requirements and ethical standards. This includes data privacy, security, and the ethical use of AI in decision-making processes.

Best Practices for Implementing AI in Operations and Supply Chain Management

To successfully integrate AI into operations and supply chain management, businesses should consider the following best practices:

1. **Develop a Clear AI Strategy**: Define specific objectives for AI implementation, such as improving demand forecasting, optimizing inventory

management, or enhancing production efficiency. Align AI initiatives with overall business goals to ensure strategic focus.

2. **Invest in Data Infrastructure**: Build robust data infrastructure to support AI applications. This includes implementing data collection, storage, and processing systems that ensure data quality and accessibility.

3. **Pilot Projects and Iteration**: Start with pilot projects to test and refine AI applications before scaling up. Use feedback and results from pilot projects to iteratively improve AI systems and ensure they meet business needs.

4. **Collaboration and Partnership**: Collaborate with AI vendors, research institutions, and industry experts to leverage external expertise and accelerate AI adoption. Partnerships can provide access to cutting-edge technologies and best practices.

5. **Employee Training and Engagement**: Provide training and support for employees to help them understand and leverage AI tools effectively. Engage employees in AI initiatives to foster a culture of innovation and continuous improvement.

6. **Monitor and Optimize**: Continuously monitor the performance of AI systems and gather feedback from users. Use this feedback to make iterative improvements and ensure AI solutions remain effective and relevant.

7. **Ensure Compliance and Ethics**: Implement measures to ensure AI applications comply with regulatory requirements and ethical standards. Regularly audit AI systems for bias and fairness, and prioritize transparency in AI decision-making processes.

AI is revolutionizing operations and supply chain management by enhancing efficiency, accuracy, and responsiveness. Through applications such as demand forecasting, inventory management, supply chain optimization, and predictive maintenance, AI enables businesses to achieve significant cost savings, improve operational performance, and better manage risks. However, successful implementation requires careful consideration of data quality, integration challenges, scalability, talent acquisition, and ethical considerations. By adopting best practices and focusing on strategic objectives, businesses can harness the transformative power of AI to drive operational excellence and maintain a competitive edge in the market.

Chapter 5: AI in Marketing and Sales

In the rapidly evolving landscape of marketing and sales, Artificial Intelligence (AI) is emerging as a transformative force. AI technologies enable businesses to reach their target audience more effectively, create personalized content, and optimize sales strategies. This chapter delves into three critical areas where AI is making a significant impact: targeted advertising and customer segmentation, AI-driven content creation, and sales forecasting and lead scoring.

Targeted Advertising and Customer Segmentation

AI is revolutionizing targeted advertising and customer segmentation by enabling more precise and personalized marketing efforts. Key AI applications in this area include:

1. **Targeted Advertising**:
   - **Behavioral Analysis**: AI algorithms analyze customer behavior across various touchpoints, including websites, social media, and purchase history. This analysis helps identify patterns and preferences, allowing marketers to create highly targeted ad campaigns. Platforms like Google Ads and Facebook

Ads use AI to deliver personalized ads based on user behavior.
   - **Contextual Advertising**: AI determines the context of a web page or app to deliver relevant ads in real-time. By understanding the content a user is engaging with, AI can place ads that are more likely to resonate with the user, enhancing engagement and conversion rates.

2. **Customer Segmentation**:
   - **Predictive Analytics**: AI leverages predictive analytics to segment customers based on their likelihood to purchase, churn, or respond to specific offers. This helps businesses prioritize high-value segments and tailor their marketing strategies accordingly.
   - **Dynamic Segmentation**: AI continuously updates customer segments based on real-time data, ensuring that marketing efforts remain relevant. Dynamic segmentation enables businesses to respond quickly to changes in customer behavior and market trends.

AI-Driven Content Creation

Content is a cornerstone of effective marketing, and AI is transforming how businesses create and manage content. Key AI applications in content creation include:

1. **Automated Content Generation**:
   - **Natural Language Generation (NLG)**: AI-powered NLG tools can generate human-like text based on data inputs. These tools are used to create product descriptions, social media posts, and even news articles. For example, platforms like OpenAI's GPT-3 can generate high-quality written content, saving time and resources.
   - **Content Personalization**: AI customizes content for individual users based on their preferences and behavior. Personalization engines recommend articles, videos, and other content tailored to each user's interests, increasing engagement and satisfaction.

2. **Enhanced Creativity and Productivity**:
   - **Idea Generation**: AI tools assist marketers in brainstorming and generating new ideas for content. By analyzing trends and customer feedback, AI can suggest relevant topics and creative angles.
   - **Content Optimization**: AI analyzes the performance of existing content and provides recommendations for optimization. This includes suggesting keywords, improving readability, and enhancing SEO to boost visibility and engagement.

Sales Forecasting and Lead Scoring

AI is transforming sales processes by providing more accurate forecasts and identifying high-potential leads. Key AI applications in sales forecasting and lead scoring include:

1. **Sales Forecasting**:
   - **Predictive Modeling**: AI uses historical sales data and market trends to predict future sales performance. This helps businesses set realistic targets, allocate resources effectively, and plan for growth. Companies like Salesforce use AI-powered tools to enhance sales forecasting accuracy.
   - **Real-Time Analytics**: AI provides real-time insights into sales performance, enabling businesses to adjust their strategies promptly. This agility is crucial for responding to market fluctuations and maintaining a competitive edge.

2. **Lead Scoring**:
   - **Behavioral Scoring**: AI analyzes the behavior of prospects, such as website visits, email interactions, and social media engagement, to assign scores indicating their likelihood to convert. This helps sales teams focus on high-potential leads and improve conversion rates.

- **Predictive Lead Scoring**: AI models evaluate various data points, including demographic information, firm graphics, and interaction history, to predict which leads are most likely to become customers. Predictive lead scoring tools like those offered by HubSpot and Marketo enhance the efficiency and effectiveness of sales efforts.

Benefits of AI in Marketing and Sales

Integrating AI into marketing and sales offers numerous benefits:

1. **Increased Personalization**: AI enables highly personalized marketing and sales strategies, enhancing customer experience and loyalty. Personalized content and targeted ads resonate more with customers, leading to higher engagement and conversion rates.

2. **Improved Efficiency**: AI automates repetitive tasks, such as content creation and lead scoring, freeing up time for marketers and sales teams to focus on strategic activities. This increases overall productivity and reduces operational costs.

3. **Enhanced Accuracy**: AI-driven analytics and predictive models provide more accurate insights and forecasts, enabling better decision-making. This helps

businesses allocate resources effectively and achieve their sales and marketing goals.

4. **Scalability**: AI systems can handle large volumes of data and interactions, making it easier to scale marketing and sales efforts. Businesses can reach and engage a larger audience without compromising quality or efficiency.

Challenges and Considerations

While AI offers significant advantages, its integration into marketing and sales also presents challenges:

1. **Data Quality and Integration**: AI systems require high-quality data to function effectively. Ensuring data accuracy, consistency, and integration across different platforms can be challenging but is essential for AI success.

2. **Privacy and Security**: Collecting and analyzing customer data raises privacy and security concerns. Businesses must comply with data protection regulations and implement robust security measures to protect customer information.

3. **Ethical Considerations**: AI-driven marketing and sales strategies must be ethical and transparent.

Businesses need to ensure that AI applications do not lead to biased or unfair practices and that customers are aware of how their data is being used.

4. **Skill Gaps**: Implementing AI requires specialized skills in data science, machine learning, and AI engineering. Businesses need to invest in training and development to build the necessary expertise within their teams.

Best Practices for Implementing AI in Marketing and Sales

To successfully integrate AI into marketing and sales, businesses should consider the following best practices:

1. **Develop a Clear AI Strategy**: Define specific objectives for AI implementation, such as improving personalization, enhancing lead scoring, or increasing content efficiency. Align AI initiatives with overall business goals to ensure strategic focus.

2. **Invest in Data Infrastructure**: Build robust data infrastructure to support AI applications. This includes implementing data collection, storage, and processing systems that ensure data quality and accessibility.

3. **Start with Pilot Projects**: Begin with pilot projects to test and refine AI applications before scaling up. Use feedback and results from pilot projects to iteratively improve AI systems and ensure they meet business needs.

4. **Focus on Customer Experience**: Prioritize AI applications that enhance customer experience, such as personalized content and targeted advertising. Ensure that AI-driven strategies are customer-centric and add value to the customer journey.

5. **Ensure Transparency and Ethics**: Implement measures to ensure AI applications are transparent and ethical. Regularly audit AI systems for bias and fairness, and communicate clearly with customers about how AI is being used.

6. **Foster Collaboration and Innovation**: Encourage collaboration between marketing, sales, and IT teams to leverage AI effectively. Foster a culture of innovation and continuous learning to keep pace with AI advancements.

AI is transforming marketing and sales by enabling targeted advertising, personalized content creation, and accurate sales forecasting. By leveraging AI technologies, businesses can enhance customer experience, improve efficiency, and achieve better outcomes. However, successful implementation requires careful consideration of data quality, privacy, ethics, and skills. By adopting best practices and focusing on customer-centric strategies, businesses can harness the power of AI to drive marketing and sales excellence in the digital age.

Chapter 6: Ethical and Legal Considerations

As AI continues to permeate various aspects of business and society, ethical and legal considerations become increasingly crucial. Ensuring data privacy and security, addressing bias and fairness in AI, and navigating the regulatory landscape are fundamental to the responsible and sustainable use of AI technologies. This chapter explores these key areas, offering insights into the challenges and best practices for ethical AI implementation.

Data Privacy and Security

Protecting data privacy and ensuring security are paramount in the AI era, where vast amounts of personal and sensitive information are processed. Key considerations and strategies include:

1. **Data Privacy**:
   - **Compliance with Regulations**: Adhering to data protection laws such as the General Data Protection Regulation (GDPR) in Europe and the California Consumer Privacy Act (CCPA) in the U.S. is essential. These regulations mandate how personal data should be collected, processed, stored, and shared, ensuring that individuals' privacy rights are protected.
   - **Informed Consent**: Obtaining explicit consent from individuals before collecting and using their data is a critical ethical practice. Transparency about how data will be used and providing users with control over their data are essential for building trust.

2. **Data Security**:
   - **Robust Security Measures**: Implementing strong security protocols, such as encryption, access controls, and regular security audits, helps protect data from breaches and unauthorized access. Businesses must stay updated with the latest security technologies and practices.
   - **Data Anonymization**: Anonymizing personal data can protect individuals' privacy while allowing for data analysis. Techniques like data masking and differential privacy ensure that sensitive information cannot be traced back to individuals.

3. **Data Governance**:
   - **Data Quality and Integrity**: Ensuring the accuracy, completeness, and consistency of data is crucial for reliable AI outcomes. Implementing robust data governance frameworks and regular data audits helps maintain data quality.
   - **Ethical Data Sourcing**: Collecting data ethically and responsibly, with respect for individuals' rights and without exploiting vulnerable populations, is essential. This includes avoiding data scraping from unauthorized sources and respecting intellectual property rights.

Ethical AI: Bias and Fairness

AI systems can inadvertently perpetuate or even exacerbate biases present in the data they are trained on. Ensuring fairness and mitigating bias are critical for ethical AI deployment:

1. **Identifying and Mitigating Bias**:
   - **Bias Detection Tools**: Utilizing AI tools designed to detect and measure bias in algorithms is crucial. These tools analyze AI outputs for disparities across different demographic groups, helping identify potential biases.
   - **Diverse Training Data**: Ensuring that training datasets are diverse and representative of the

populations they will impact helps reduce bias. This includes considering factors like race, gender, age, and socioeconomic status.

2. **Fairness in AI**:
   - **Algorithmic Fairness**: Developing and implementing algorithms that treat all individuals fairly and equitably is essential. Techniques such as fairness constraints and regular audits can help ensure that AI systems do not discriminate.
   - **Transparent AI Models**: Providing transparency in AI decision-making processes helps build trust and accountability. Explainable AI (XAI) techniques allow users to understand how decisions are made and identify any potential biases.

3. **Ethical Frameworks and Guidelines**:
   - **Ethical AI Principles**: Adopting ethical AI principles, such as those outlined by organizations like the IEEE or the Partnership on AI, provides a foundation for responsible AI use. These principles often include fairness, accountability, transparency, and human-centric values.
   - **AI Ethics Committees**: Establishing ethics committees to oversee AI projects and ensure adherence to ethical standards can help address ethical concerns proactively. These committees should include diverse stakeholders to provide varied perspectives.

Regulatory Landscape for AI

Navigating the complex and evolving regulatory landscape for AI is critical for compliance and ethical AI deployment:

1. **Global AI Regulations**:
   - **GDPR and CCPA**: These regulations set stringent requirements for data protection and privacy, impacting how AI systems handle personal data. Compliance with these laws is essential for businesses operating in Europe and California.
   - **AI-Specific Regulations**: Countries like the EU are developing AI-specific regulations, such as the proposed EU Artificial Intelligence Act, which aims to ensure the safe and ethical use of AI. Staying informed about such developments is crucial for global businesses.

2. **Industry Standards and Guidelines**:
   - **ISO/IEC Standards**: International standards like ISO/IEC 27001 for information security management and ISO/IEC 27701 for privacy information management provide frameworks for managing data security and privacy in AI systems.
   - **Sector-Specific Guidelines**: Different industries may have specific guidelines and best practices for AI

use. For example, the healthcare sector has guidelines for AI in medical devices, ensuring patient safety and efficacy.

3. **Legal Compliance and Risk Management**:
   - **Compliance Programs**: Implementing comprehensive compliance programs that address data protection, privacy, and ethical AI practices helps mitigate legal risks. Regular training and awareness programs ensure that employees understand and adhere to these practices.
   - **Legal Counsel and Consultation**: Engaging legal experts who specialize in AI and data protection can provide valuable guidance on navigating regulatory requirements and mitigating legal risks.

Best Practices for Ethical and Legal AI Implementation

To ensure ethical and legal compliance in AI deployment, businesses should adopt the following best practices:

1. **Develop an Ethical AI Strategy**: Define clear ethical guidelines for AI use, aligned with business values and regulatory requirements. Ensure that ethical considerations are integrated into every stage of AI development and deployment.

2. **Implement Strong Data Governance**: Establish robust data governance frameworks to ensure data quality, privacy, and security. Regularly audit data practices and update policies to reflect the latest standards and regulations.

3. **Foster Transparency and Accountability**: Provide transparency in AI decision-making processes and ensure accountability for AI outcomes. Use explainable AI techniques and communicate clearly with stakeholders about how AI is being used.

4. **Engage Diverse Stakeholders**: Involve diverse stakeholders in AI projects, including ethicists, legal experts, and representatives from impacted communities. This helps ensure that multiple perspectives are considered and ethical concerns are addressed.

5. **Invest in Training and Education**: Provide ongoing training for employees on data protection, ethical AI practices, and regulatory compliance. Foster a culture of continuous learning and awareness about ethical and legal considerations in AI.

6. **Monitor and Evaluate AI Systems**: Continuously monitor AI systems for performance, bias, and compliance with ethical standards. Use feedback loops

to iteratively improve AI systems and address any emerging ethical or legal issues.

As AI becomes increasingly integral to business operations, addressing ethical and legal considerations is paramount. Ensuring data privacy and security, mitigating bias and ensuring fairness, and navigating the regulatory landscape are critical for responsible AI use. By adopting best practices and fostering a culture of ethical AI, businesses can leverage AI technologies while safeguarding individual rights and maintaining public trust. This proactive approach to ethical and legal AI implementation will be essential for sustainable success in the AI-driven future.

Chapter 7: The Future of Work with AI

The advent of AI is reshaping the workplace, creating a complex landscape where job displacement coexists with job creation. As AI automates routine tasks and enhances productivity, it simultaneously generates new opportunities and demands new skills. This chapter explores the dual impact of AI on jobs, the role of AI in workforce management, and the critical skills required for the future workforce.

Job Displacement vs. Job Creation

AI's impact on employment is multifaceted, encompassing both the displacement of existing jobs and the creation of new ones. Understanding this dynamic is crucial for businesses and workers alike.

1. **Job Displacement**:
    - **Automation of Routine Tasks**: AI and robotics are increasingly capable of performing repetitive and mundane tasks, leading to the displacement of roles in manufacturing, data entry, customer service, and more. For example, the rise of AI-driven chatbots has reduced the demand for human customer service representatives.
    - **Restructuring of Job Roles**: AI's ability to analyze data and perform complex calculations can lead to the redefinition of job roles. Jobs that primarily involve data analysis, financial forecasting, and certain administrative tasks may be restructured to leverage AI capabilities, potentially reducing the need for human involvement in these areas.

2. **Job Creation**:
    - **Emergence of New Roles**: AI technology itself requires the creation of new job roles such as AI specialists, data scientists, machine learning engineers, and AI ethicists. These roles focus on developing, managing, and overseeing AI systems.

- **Enhancement of Human Roles**: AI augments human capabilities, leading to the evolution of existing roles. For instance, in healthcare, AI assists doctors by providing diagnostic support, allowing them to focus on patient care and complex decision-making.

3. **Economic and Sectoral Shifts**:
   - **Sectoral Growth**: Certain sectors, such as technology, healthcare, and finance, are experiencing growth due to AI advancements. These sectors are likely to see a surge in job opportunities related to AI development, implementation, and maintenance.
   - **Economic Impact**: While AI may lead to short-term job displacement, it also has the potential to boost economic productivity and create long-term employment opportunities by fostering innovation and new business models.

AI in Workforce Management

AI is transforming workforce management by enhancing recruitment processes, optimizing employee performance, and facilitating better decision-making.

1. **Recruitment and Talent Acquisition**:
   - **AI-Powered Recruiting Tools**: AI-driven platforms streamline the recruitment process by analyzing resumes, conducting initial screenings, and

matching candidates with suitable roles. Tools like HireVue and Pymetrics use AI to assess candidates' skills and fit, improving hiring efficiency and accuracy.
   - **Bias Reduction**: AI can help reduce unconscious bias in recruitment by focusing on skills and qualifications rather than demographic factors. However, it is crucial to ensure that AI systems themselves are free from bias.

2. **Performance Management and Employee Engagement**:
   - **Personalized Training and Development**: AI analyzes employee performance data to identify skill gaps and recommend personalized training programs. Platforms like LinkedIn Learning use AI to suggest relevant courses based on employees' career goals and learning preferences.
   - **Employee Engagement**: AI tools monitor employee sentiment through surveys and feedback analysis, helping managers understand and improve workplace morale. AI-driven engagement platforms like CultureAmp provide insights into employee satisfaction and areas for improvement.

3. **Decision-Making and Workforce Planning**:
   - **Predictive Analytics**: AI leverages predictive analytics to forecast workforce trends, such as turnover rates and talent shortages. This enables businesses to

make proactive decisions about hiring, training, and workforce allocation.
   - **Resource Optimization**: AI helps optimize resource allocation by analyzing project requirements and matching them with available skills and personnel. This ensures that the right talent is assigned to the right tasks, enhancing productivity and efficiency.

Skills for the Future: Preparing the Workforce

As AI transforms the nature of work, preparing the workforce with the necessary skills and competencies becomes imperative.

1. **Technical Skills**:
   - **AI and Machine Learning**: Understanding AI fundamentals, machine learning algorithms, and data science is increasingly valuable. Courses and certifications in AI and related fields can provide a solid foundation for workers.
   - **Data Literacy**: Proficiency in data analysis, data visualization, and statistical methods is essential for leveraging AI insights. Familiarity with tools like Python, R, and SQL is beneficial for data-related roles.

2. **Soft Skills**:
   - **Adaptability and Continuous Learning**: The ability to adapt to new technologies and continuously

learn new skills is critical in an AI-driven workplace. Lifelong learning and professional development are key to staying relevant.
   - **Critical Thinking and Problem-Solving**: AI can augment decision-making, but human critical thinking and problem-solving skills remain indispensable. Workers need to interpret AI-generated insights and make informed decisions.

3. **Human-Centric Skills**:
   - **Emotional Intelligence**: As AI takes over routine tasks, human roles will increasingly focus on interpersonal interactions and emotional intelligence. Skills in communication, empathy, and collaboration will be crucial.
   - **Ethics and Governance**: Understanding the ethical implications of AI and being able to navigate its regulatory landscape is essential. Training in AI ethics, data privacy, and compliance will become increasingly important.

4. **Interdisciplinary Knowledge**:
   - **Integration of AI with Domain Expertise**: Workers who can integrate AI knowledge with expertise in specific domains, such as healthcare, finance, or manufacturing, will be highly valuable. This interdisciplinary approach enables the practical application of AI to solve real-world problems.

Best Practices for Workforce Transition

To facilitate a smooth transition to an AI-enhanced workforce, businesses should adopt the following best practices:

1. **Invest in Training and Upskilling**: Provide employees with access to training programs, online courses, and certifications in AI, data science, and related fields. Encourage continuous learning and professional development.

2. **Foster a Culture of Innovation**: Cultivate a workplace culture that embraces innovation and experimentation. Encourage employees to explore new technologies and apply AI in creative ways to solve business challenges.

3. **Promote Collaboration between Humans and AI**: Develop strategies that promote collaboration between human workers and AI systems. Emphasize the complementary nature of AI and human skills, and design workflows that leverage the strengths of both.

4. **Ensure Ethical AI Practices**: Implement policies and frameworks to ensure the ethical use of AI. Regularly audit AI systems for bias and fairness, and

involve diverse stakeholders in AI governance to address ethical concerns.

5. **Support Workforce Transition**: Provide support for employees whose roles may be impacted by AI. This includes offering career counseling, job placement services, and transition programs to help workers find new opportunities within or outside the organization.

The future of work with AI presents both challenges and opportunities. While AI-driven automation may displace certain jobs, it also creates new roles and enhances existing ones. By leveraging AI in workforce management and preparing employees with the necessary skills, businesses can navigate this transition effectively. Investing in training, fostering a culture of innovation, and ensuring ethical AI practices are key to harnessing the potential of AI while supporting the workforce in an evolving job landscape. As AI continues to shape the future of work, proactive and strategic approaches will be essential for sustainable success and growth.

Chapter 8: Strategic Planning for AI Implementation

Strategic planning is essential for successful AI implementation in organizations. Developing a comprehensive AI strategy, fostering a culture that embraces AI, and establishing measurable success metrics are critical components of effective AI deployment. This chapter explores strategies for developing and executing AI implementation plans.

Developing an AI Strategy

1. **Assess Organizational Needs and Objectives**:
   - Identify key business challenges and opportunities where AI can make a significant impact. This may include improving operational efficiency, enhancing customer experience, or driving innovation.
   - Align AI initiatives with overall organizational goals and priorities to ensure strategic focus and resource allocation.

2. **Define Clear Objectives and KPIs**:
   - Establish specific, measurable, achievable, relevant, and time-bound (SMART) objectives for AI implementation. These objectives should align with business outcomes and serve as benchmarks for success.
   - Define key performance indicators (KPIs) and metrics to track progress and evaluate the effectiveness of AI initiatives. Common KPIs include

ROI, cost savings, revenue growth, and customer satisfaction.

3. **Assess AI Readiness and Capabilities**:
   - Evaluate the organization's readiness for AI adoption, including technical infrastructure, data readiness, and talent availability.
   - Identify existing AI capabilities within the organization and areas where additional expertise or resources may be needed.

4. **Develop a Roadmap for Implementation**:
   - Create a detailed roadmap outlining the steps and timeline for AI implementation. This roadmap should include milestones, resource requirements, and dependencies.
   - Prioritize AI projects based on their potential impact and feasibility, considering factors such as complexity, resource availability, and alignment with strategic objectives.

Building an AI-Ready Culture

1. **Leadership Commitment and Support**:
   - Secure leadership buy-in and commitment to AI initiatives. Leaders should champion AI adoption, allocate resources, and create a supportive environment for experimentation and innovation.

- Communicate the strategic importance of AI to all stakeholders and emphasize the organization's commitment to driving digital transformation through AI.

2. **Promote Cross-Functional Collaboration**:
   - Foster collaboration between different departments and teams to leverage diverse perspectives and expertise in AI implementation.
   - Create interdisciplinary AI teams comprising data scientists, domain experts, engineers, and business analysts to ensure holistic and effective solutions.

3. **Encourage Experimentation and Learning**:
   - Encourage a culture of experimentation and learning where employees are empowered to explore AI technologies and ideas.
   - Provide training and development opportunities to build AI skills and literacy across the organization. This may include workshops, online courses, and hands-on projects.

4. **Embrace Agility and Adaptability**:
   - Embrace agile methodologies and iterative approaches to AI development and deployment. This allows for rapid experimentation, feedback, and adjustment based on real-world outcomes.

- Encourage flexibility and adaptability to navigate uncertainties and challenges inherent in AI implementation.

Measuring AI Success: KPIs and Metrics

1. **Business Impact Metrics**:
   - Measure the business impact of AI initiatives using KPIs such as ROI, revenue growth, cost savings, and market share.
   - Track improvements in key business processes, such as customer acquisition, retention, and satisfaction, attributable to AI implementation.

2. **Operational Efficiency Metrics**:
   - Assess the impact of AI on operational efficiency metrics, including process cycle time, resource utilization, and error rates.
   - Monitor changes in productivity, throughput, and quality resulting from AI-driven process improvements.

3. **Customer Experience Metrics**:
   - Evaluate the impact of AI on customer experience using metrics such as Net Promoter Score (NPS), customer satisfaction (CSAT), and customer lifetime value (CLV).

- Track improvements in personalized recommendations, response times, and overall satisfaction driven by AI-powered interactions.

4. **AI Performance Metrics**:
   - Measure the performance of AI models and algorithms using metrics such as accuracy, precision, recall, and F1 score.
   - Monitor model drift, bias, and fairness over time to ensure the reliability and fairness of AI systems.

Strategic planning is essential for successful AI implementation in organizations. By developing a comprehensive AI strategy, fostering an AI-ready culture, and establishing measurable success metrics, businesses can drive successful AI adoption and achieve tangible outcomes. Leadership commitment, cross-functional collaboration, experimentation, and adaptability are key enablers of AI success. By aligning AI initiatives with business objectives, investing in talent and capabilities, and continuously measuring and refining AI performance, organizations can unlock the full potential of AI to drive innovation, efficiency, and competitive advantage.

Chapter 9: Industry-Specific AI Applications

AI is revolutionizing various industries by driving innovation, optimizing processes, and enhancing decision-making. This chapter explores industry-specific applications of AI in healthcare, finance, retail, and manufacturing, highlighting the transformative impact of AI technologies.

AI in Healthcare

1. **Medical Imaging and Diagnostics**:
   - AI-powered image recognition algorithms assist radiologists in interpreting medical images, such as X-rays, MRIs, and CT scans, with greater accuracy and efficiency.
   - Deep learning models analyze imaging data to detect abnormalities, tumors, and other medical conditions at an early stage, facilitating timely diagnosis and treatment.

2. **Drug Discovery and Development**:
   - AI accelerates the drug discovery process by analyzing vast amounts of biological data and identifying potential drug candidates.
   - Machine learning algorithms predict the efficacy and safety of drug compounds, helping pharmaceutical companies prioritize promising candidates for further research and clinical trials.

3. **Personalized Medicine and Treatment Planning**:
   - AI algorithms analyze patient data, including genetic information, medical history, and lifestyle factors, to tailor treatment plans and interventions to individual patients.
   - Predictive analytics models forecast disease progression and treatment outcomes, enabling healthcare providers to deliver personalized care and optimize patient outcomes.

AI in Finance

1. **Algorithmic Trading and Financial Forecasting**:
   - AI-powered trading algorithms analyze market data in real-time to identify trading opportunities and execute transactions with speed and precision.
   - Predictive analytics models forecast market trends, asset prices, and risk factors, enabling investors and financial institutions to make informed investment decisions.

2. **Fraud Detection and Risk Management**:
   - AI systems detect fraudulent activities and suspicious transactions by analyzing patterns and anomalies in financial data.
   - Machine learning models assess credit risk, identify potential defaults, and optimize loan approval

processes, improving the accuracy and efficiency of risk management.

3. **Customer Service and Personal Finance Management**:
   - Chatbots and virtual assistants powered by AI provide personalized financial advice, answer customer queries, and assist with account management.
   - Natural language processing (NLP) algorithms analyze customer interactions and sentiment to enhance customer service experiences and loyalty.

AI in Retail

1. **Demand Forecasting and Inventory Management**:
   - AI algorithms analyze historical sales data, market trends, and external factors to predict consumer demand and optimize inventory levels.
   - Machine learning models optimize replenishment strategies, minimize stockouts, and reduce excess inventory, improving operational efficiency and profitability.

2. **Personalized Marketing and Customer Experience**:
   - AI-powered recommendation engines analyze customer behavior, preferences, and purchase history

to deliver personalized product recommendations and promotions.
   - Natural language processing (NLP) algorithms analyze customer feedback and sentiment on social media and review platforms to enhance brand perception and loyalty.

3. **Supply Chain Optimization and Logistics**:
   - AI optimizes supply chain processes, route planning, and warehouse operations to minimize costs, reduce lead times, and improve delivery performance.
   - Predictive analytics models forecast demand variability, supply disruptions, and transportation delays, enabling retailers to proactively mitigate risks and optimize resource allocation.

AI in Manufacturing

1. **Predictive Maintenance and Equipment Optimization**:
   - AI algorithms analyze sensor data, equipment telemetry, and historical maintenance records to predict equipment failures and schedule maintenance activities proactively.
   - Machine learning models optimize production schedules, minimize downtime, and extend the lifespan of machinery and assets, improving overall equipment effectiveness (OEE).

2. **Quality Control and Defect Detection**:
   - AI-powered computer vision systems inspect products and components for defects, deviations, and anomalies with high accuracy and speed.
   - Deep learning models classify and categorize defects, identify root causes, and recommend corrective actions, reducing scrap rates and improving product quality.

3. **Process Optimization and Automation**:
   - AI optimizes manufacturing processes, production workflows, and resource utilization to increase efficiency, reduce waste, and lower production costs.
   - Robotic process automation (RPA) automates repetitive tasks, such as data entry, assembly, and packaging, freeing up human workers for higher-value activities and innovation.

AI is transforming industries across healthcare, finance, retail, and manufacturing by driving innovation, optimizing processes, and enhancing decision-making. In healthcare, AI improves medical imaging, drug discovery, and personalized treatment. In finance, AI powers algorithmic trading, fraud detection, and customer service. In retail, AI enables demand forecasting, personalized marketing, and supply chain optimization. In manufacturing, AI drives predictive maintenance, quality control, and process automation. By leveraging AI technologies, businesses can gain a competitive edge, deliver value to customers, and drive sustainable growth in the digital age.

Chapter 10: Emerging Trends and Future Directions

As AI continues to evolve, it intersects with emerging technologies and trends, shaping the future of various industries. This chapter explores the convergence of AI with the Internet of Things (IoT), quantum computing, blockchain, and its role in fostering sustainable business practices.

AI and the Internet of Things (IoT)

1. **Integration for Smart Systems**:
   - AI enhances IoT devices and systems by enabling intelligent data analysis, predictive maintenance, and automated decision-making.
   - IoT sensors collect vast amounts of data from connected devices, which AI algorithms analyze to derive actionable insights and optimize operations.

2. **Edge Computing and AI**:

- Edge AI brings AI processing closer to IoT devices, reducing latency and improving real-time decision-making.
- AI algorithms deployed at the edge analyze data locally, enabling faster response times and reducing bandwidth requirements.

3. **Predictive Maintenance and Anomaly Detection**:
   - AI-powered predictive maintenance models analyze IoT sensor data to anticipate equipment failures and schedule maintenance proactively.
   - Anomaly detection algorithms identify deviations from normal operating conditions, enabling early detection of issues and minimizing downtime.

Quantum Computing and AI

1. **Potential for Exponential Speedup**:
   - Quantum computing has the potential to significantly accelerate AI algorithms, especially those involving optimization, simulation, and pattern recognition.
   - Quantum algorithms can solve certain AI problems exponentially faster than classical computers, unlocking new capabilities and applications.

2. **Optimization and Machine Learning**:

- Quantum computing algorithms can optimize complex AI models and machine learning processes, enabling faster training and inference.
   - Quantum machine learning techniques leverage quantum principles to enhance pattern recognition, data clustering, and classification tasks.

3. **Challenges and Opportunities**:
   - Quantum computing is still in its early stages, with practical challenges such as qubit stability, error correction, and scalability.
   - Collaboration between AI and quantum computing researchers can accelerate progress and unlock new frontiers in artificial intelligence.

AI and Blockchain: Potential Synergies

1. **Enhanced Security and Privacy**:
   - Blockchain technology provides a decentralized and tamper-resistant framework for securing AI data, transactions, and models.
   - AI algorithms can analyze blockchain data to detect anomalies, verify transactions, and ensure data integrity.

2. **Decentralized AI Marketplaces**:

- Blockchain-based platforms enable the creation of decentralized AI marketplaces where users can buy, sell, and trade AI algorithms, datasets, and services.
- Smart contracts facilitate transparent and automated transactions, ensuring trust and fairness in AI exchanges.

3. **Data Sharing and Collaboration**:
   - Blockchain allows for secure and auditable data sharing among multiple parties, enabling collaborative AI initiatives while preserving data privacy and ownership.
   - Federated learning techniques leverage blockchain to facilitate distributed model training across multiple devices and organizations without sharing raw data.

The Role of AI in Sustainable Business Practices

1. **Environmental Impact Reduction**:
   - AI technologies help optimize energy consumption, resource utilization, and supply chain logistics, reducing the environmental footprint of businesses.
   - Predictive analytics and optimization algorithms enable more efficient resource allocation and waste reduction, contributing to sustainability goals.

2. **Renewable Energy Optimization**:

- AI algorithms optimize renewable energy generation, storage, and distribution, maximizing the efficiency and reliability of solar, wind, and other renewable sources.
- Predictive models forecast energy demand and supply fluctuations, enabling better management of renewable energy resources.

3. **Eco-friendly Manufacturing and Operations**:
   - AI-driven process optimization and automation reduce waste, emissions, and energy consumption in manufacturing and industrial operations.
   - AI-powered predictive maintenance minimizes downtime and extends the lifespan of equipment, reducing the need for resource-intensive replacements.

The convergence of AI with emerging technologies such as IoT, quantum computing, and blockchain presents exciting opportunities for innovation and transformation across industries. By leveraging AI in conjunction with these technologies, businesses can unlock new capabilities, improve efficiency, and drive sustainable practices. As AI continues to evolve, its role in shaping the future of technology and business will be central to driving progress and addressing complex challenges in the digital age.

Conclusion: Navigating the AI-Driven Future

The Continuous Evolution of AI

The journey of artificial intelligence (AI) is marked by continuous evolution, innovation, and transformation. From its early beginnings as a concept to its current state as a pervasive technology shaping various aspects of society, AI has undergone remarkable advancements and breakthroughs. As AI technologies continue to evolve, they hold the promise of revolutionizing industries, driving economic growth, and addressing complex societal challenges.

Preparing for a Future with AI

Navigating the AI-driven future requires proactive preparation and strategic foresight. Organizations and individuals must embrace AI as a transformative force and invest in the necessary skills, capabilities, and infrastructure to harness its potential. This entails:

1. **Investing in Talent and Expertise**: Organizations should prioritize talent acquisition and development in AI-related fields, including data science, machine learning, and AI ethics. Continuous learning and upskilling programs are essential to equip the

workforce with the skills required to thrive in an AI-driven environment.

2. **Embracing Ethical AI Practices**: Ethical considerations must be at the forefront of AI development and deployment. Organizations should adopt ethical AI principles, promote transparency and accountability, and mitigate bias and discrimination in AI systems. Collaboration between policymakers, industry leaders, and ethicists is crucial to ensure the responsible and equitable use of AI.

3. **Fostering Innovation and Collaboration**: Innovation thrives in environments that encourage experimentation, collaboration, and diversity of thought. Organizations should create ecosystems that foster innovation, facilitate knowledge sharing, and embrace interdisciplinary collaboration across sectors and disciplines.

4. **Adapting to Technological Change**: The pace of technological change is accelerating, and organizations must adapt quickly to stay competitive. Agility, flexibility, and adaptability are key attributes that enable organizations to navigate uncertain and dynamic environments. Embracing emerging technologies, such as AI, IoT, and blockchain, can unlock new opportunities for growth and innovation.

Final Thoughts and Recommendations

As we stand on the brink of a new era defined by AI, it is essential to approach the future with optimism, curiosity, and responsibility. AI has the potential to empower individuals, enhance productivity, and drive positive societal change. However, realizing this potential requires collective effort, collaboration, and a shared commitment to ethical and inclusive AI practices.

In conclusion, navigating the AI-driven future is a journey filled with opportunities, challenges, and possibilities. By embracing AI as a transformative force, investing in talent and expertise, fostering innovation and collaboration, and prioritizing ethical considerations, we can harness the full potential of AI to create a brighter, more inclusive future for all. As we embark on this journey, let us embrace the possibilities of AI while remaining steadfast in our commitment to building a sustainable and equitable future for generations to come.

EPILOGUE:

As we come to the conclusion of this journey through the realms of artificial intelligence (AI) and its profound impact on business and society, we are reminded of the immense potential and responsibility that accompany the advancements in this field.

The landscape of AI is ever-changing, with new technologies, applications, and ethical considerations continually shaping its trajectory. Yet, amidst the complexities and uncertainties, one thing remains clear: AI has the power to drive unprecedented innovation, transformation, and progress.

In this epilogue, we reflect on the key themes and insights explored throughout this book and offer some final thoughts on the future of AI and its implications for humanity.

1. **The Promise of AI**: AI holds the promise of unlocking new frontiers in productivity, efficiency, and human ingenuity. From revolutionizing healthcare and finance to transforming retail and manufacturing, AI has the potential to reshape industries and improve the quality of life for people around the world.

2. **The Importance of Ethics**: As AI technologies become more pervasive and impactful, the need for ethical AI practices becomes paramount. It is essential to prioritize transparency, accountability, and fairness in AI development and deployment to ensure that AI benefits society as a whole.

3. **The Role of Human-Centric AI**: While AI can augment human capabilities and improve decision-making, it is essential to remember that humans must remain at the center of AI development and use. Human judgment, empathy, and ethical reasoning are irreplaceable assets in navigating the complex ethical and societal implications of AI.

4. **The Journey Ahead**: As we look to the future, the journey through the AI-driven landscape is filled with both opportunities and challenges. It is up to us, as individuals, organizations, and society as a whole, to chart a course that maximizes the benefits of AI while mitigating risks and ensuring inclusivity and equity for all.

In closing, let us approach the future with optimism, curiosity, and responsibility. Let us embrace the possibilities of AI while remaining steadfast in our commitment to ethical and human-centered innovation.

Together, let us embark on this journey into the AI-driven future with courage, wisdom, and foresight.

[Kenneth Christopher]

SUMMARY:

In this comprehensive exploration of artificial intelligence (AI) and its impact on business, society, and humanity, we have delved into the evolution, applications, and future directions of AI. From its humble beginnings to its current state as a transformative force, AI has revolutionized industries, reshaped workflows, and redefined human interactions.

Throughout the chapters, we have examined the role of AI in various sectors, including healthcare, finance, retail, and manufacturing, highlighting its applications in medical imaging, algorithmic trading, personalized marketing, predictive maintenance, and more. We have explored the strategic planning for AI implementation, the ethical considerations of AI adoption, and the emerging trends shaping the future, such as the convergence of AI with the Internet of Things (IoT), quantum computing, and blockchain.

Key themes that have emerged include the promise of AI to drive innovation and efficiency, the importance of ethical AI practices to ensure transparency and fairness, and the need for human-centric approaches to AI development and use. As we navigate the AI-driven future, it is essential to prioritize collaboration, innovation, and responsible AI governance to maximize the benefits of AI while mitigating risks and ensuring inclusivity and equity for all.

In conclusion, the journey through the field of AI is filled with opportunities, challenges, and possibilities. By embracing the transformative potential of AI while upholding ethical principles and human values, we can navigate the complexities of the AI landscape and shape a future that harnesses the power of AI for the betterment of humanity.

[Kenneth Christopher]

www.ingramcontent.com/pod-product-compliance
Lightning Source LLC
Chambersburg PA
CBHW082212220526
45470CB00010B/3140